Doing the Right Thing

Making Responsible Decisions

BY ALYSSA KREKELBERG

The Child's World®
childsworld.com

Published by The Child's World®
1980 Lookout Drive • Mankato, MN 56003-1705
800-599-READ • www.childsworld.com

Photographs ©: Robert Kneschke/Shutterstock
Images, cover, 1, 10, 13, 14; iStockphoto, 5, 6, 9;
Sergey Novikov/Shutterstock Images, 17, 18, 21

ISBN 9781503844506 (Reinforced Library Binding)
ISBN 9781503846739 (Portable Document Format)
ISBN 9781503847927 (Online Multi-user eBook)
LCCN 2019956609

Printed in the United States of America

ABOUT THE AUTHOR

Alyssa Krekelberg is a
children's book editor
and author. She lives
in Minnesota with her
hyper husky.

Contents

CHAPTER ONE

Making a Mistake

Harper and her parents are at the store. Harper is **upset** because her parents will not buy her any candy. She starts to scream and stomp her feet. Other people in the store turn to look at her.

Sometimes you might act out without thinking first.

Screaming at people is not a good way to communicate.

Harper's parents are **disappointed** in her actions, which makes Harper feel sad. She **regrets** her decision. She knows that screaming will not get her what she wants.

"What could you have done differently?" her mom asks.

Harper thinks about it. She should have calmly told her parents that she did not like their decision. Even though she may not have changed their minds, speaking calmly would have been a better decision than screaming.

People should always think about how their actions affect others.

It is important to talk to your friends before touching their things.

CHAPTER TWO

Fixing a Bad Decision

Drew wants to play soccer, but his friend, Micah, has the ball. Drew does not ask if he can play. Instead, he takes the ball from Micah.

"That was my ball! Give it back!" Micah says.

Drew thinks about how he made Micah feel. Micah is sad. Drew wants to **apologize** to his friend and make up for his bad decision.

"I am sorry," Drew says. "I should not have taken your ball."

Sometimes it is hard to think of a better choice at first.

How would you solve
a fight with a friend?

Micah **forgives** Drew for taking the ball. He smiles and gives Drew a hug.

"Can we play soccer together?" Drew asks.

"Yes!" Micah says.

THINK ABOUT IT!

Think of a time when you made a bad decision. How did it hurt the people around you?

Why should people think about how their actions will affect others?

CHAPTER THREE

A Good Choice

Nick is at the park with his friend Gina. They are having fun. First they play together on the swings. Then Gina pushes Nick on his skateboard.

Later, other kids ask Nick if he wants to play with them. They have different games to play. They are laughing and having fun.

The park is a great place to make new friends.

Try to think about how other people might feel.

18

Nick thinks about how Gina would feel if he left and played with other kids instead of her. Gina would be upset. She might even cry. Nick does not want to leave Gina behind.

"Can we all play together?" Nick asks the other kids. They say yes. Everyone runs to the seesaw. Gina and Nick both have fun. The kids all get along on the playground.

When you make good decisions, other people are happy.

GLOSSARY

apologize (uh-PAWL-oh-jize) To apologize is to say you are sorry for hurting someone. Drew wanted to apologize to Micah for stealing the soccer ball.

disappointed (dis-uh-POYNT-ed) To be disappointed is to feel let down. Harper's parents were disappointed with how she behaved.

forgives (fur-GIVZ) If someone forgives you, that means he or she has stopped being mad at you for a mistake. Drew's friend forgives him.

regrets (ree-GRETZ) If someone regrets something, that means he or she feels sad about it. Harper regrets screaming in the store.

upset (up-SET) Someone who is upset is unhappy. Harper was upset after she made a bad choice.

Books

Dinmont, Kerry. *Angry*. Mankato, MN:
The Child's World, 2019.

Milgrim, David. *Wild Feelings*. New York, NY:
Henry Holt and Company, 2015.

Smith, Bryan. *What Were You Thinking?*
A Story about Learning to Control Your Impulses.
Boys Town, NE: Boys Town Press, 2016.

Websites

Visit our website for links about making
responsible decisions:
childsworld.com/links

*Note to Parents, Teachers, and Librarians: We routinely verify our Web links to make
sure they are safe and active sites. So encourage your readers to check them out!*

INDEX